JEANNIEOLOGY

JEANNIE BERGLAND

To order additional copies of this book, contact:
Xlibris
844-714-8691
www.Xlibris.com
Orders@Xlibris.com

ISBN: 978-1-6641-3101-9 (sc)
ISBN: 978-1-6641-3100-2 (e)

Print information available on the last page

Rev. date: 11/06/2020

CONTENTS

SPECIAL THANKS

I want to take time to give thanks to God,
to my family and friends.
A special thanks to my husband Robin, for one of his drawings
and my daughter, Julie, for the beautiful cloud photo.
For my friend, Nancy Beck for helping me edit my book.
My family and friends for their support and extra push
when I needed it.

INTRODUCTION

This is my very first published Bible Study on the "End Times". I have two other books out: "Jeannie's Gems" (Poetry book), and "God's Little Bush" (Children's Book). I started the first two chapters with a written prayer. After thinking about this, I thought that it would be best if people would say their own prayers before starting each chapter. This is to be a study where we are open to God's Holy Spirit and God's Holy Word. The Bible has a **lot** to say concerning the times we are living in now and the times to come.

I firmly believe that, God's Holy Bible is the infallible Word of God, that's why I am doing this "Bible Study". My desire is that everyone who does this study will read, study, pray, and think about all the evidence given in the scriptures concerning the "End Times" and not be deceived. God does not want us to be deceived.

Now, let's dive into His Holy Word!

Jeannieology: Sealed to Revealed

CHAPTER 1

*"...for the words are closed up and **sealed** till the time of the end."*
Daniel 12:9

Dear Heavenly Father,
We thank You for loving us and giving us Your Son to purchase our salvation, healing, deliverance, and everything we need for life and godliness. We thank You, for Your Holy Spirit, who will lead us into all Truth. As we humbly, and boldly, come before You to seek out Your Truth concerning the last days, and the sign of Your Son's soon return. We want to be ready, watching, and praying, as your Holy Word has instructed us to do so. We do not want to be decieved . Thank You for hearing and answering our prayers, in the name of Jesus we ask this – Amen.

The name of this book is called "Sealed to Revealed" because I want to show you the scriptures that were once "sealed", and now, in these latter times, have been revealed. But first, let's look at what the word "sealed" means in the Bible, starting with Isaiah:

Isaiah 29:11,12 "And the vision of all is become unto you as the words of a book that is **sealed**, which *men* deliver to one that is learned, saying, Read this, I pray thee: and he saith, I cannot; for it *is* **sealed**: And the book is delivered to him that is not learned, saying, Read this, I pray thee: and he saith, I am not learned."

sealed (H 2856) ; çÈúÇí **châtham,** khaw-tham'; a primitive root; to close up; especially to seal:—make an end, mark, seal (up), stop.

(All Hebrew & Greek definitions will be from the : wwwblueletterbible.org; unless, otherwise indicated)

1. **sealed** (https://www.thefreedictionary.com/sealed): seal 1 n.:
1.
a. A device or material that is used to close off or fasten an opening or connection, especially to prevent the escape of a liquid or gas: *used caulk as a seal around the window.*
    b. An airtight closure: *a door that lacks a tight seal.*
    c. Something, such as a piece of tape, that is placed on a product or package to show that the contents have not been tampered with.
    d. The water in the trap of a drain that prevents sewer gas from escaping into a room.

2.
a. A design used to identify a person or thing or to show that something is authentic, accurate, or of good quality: *The title page is <u>marked</u> with the publisher's seal. Does the scale have the inspector's seal?*
    b. A small decorative paper sticker.

3.

a. A die or signet having a raised or incised emblem used to stamp an impression on a receptive substance such as wax or lead.

    b. The impression so made.

    c. The design or emblem itself, belonging exclusively to the user: *a monarch's seal.*

    d. A small disk or <u>wafer</u> of wax, lead, or paper bearing such an imprint and affixed to a document to prove authenticity or to secure it.

4. An indication or symbol regarded as guaranteeing or authenticating something: *The choral director gave the program his seal of approval.*

tr. v. : sealed, sealling, seals:

1. **a.** To close or fasten with a seal: *seal an envelope; seal a test tube.*

    b. To prevent (a liquid or gas) from escaping: *Charring a piece of meat seals in the juices.*

    c. To cover, secure, or fill up (an opening): *sealed the hole in the pipe with epoxy.*

    d. To apply a waterproof coating to: *seal a blacktop driveway.*

    e. To secure or prevent passage into and out of (an area). Often used with *off: The police sealed off the crime scene.*

2. **To affix a seal to (something) in order to prove authenticity, accuracy, or quality.**

3. **To establish or determine** <u>**irrevocably**</u>: *Our fate was sealed.*

...

"Then opened he their understanding, that they might understand the scriptures,"
Luke 24:45

"*Even* the mystery which hath been hid from ages and from generations, but now is made manifest to His saints: To whom God would make known what *is* the riches of the glory of this mystery among the Gentiles; which is Christ in you, the hope of glory:"
Colossians 1:26,27

We now know the mystery of salvation through Jesus Christ. There have been many hidden things in the scriptures, that have now been revealed to us: we have the written Holy Word of God and we have His Holy Spirit in us, if we have invited Jesus Christ into our hearts and made Him the Lord of our lives. If we have questions for Him we can ask Him in prayer, and He will answer us. Sometimes, we are not able to handle the answers right away (John 16:12); but, He will answer us, when the time is right.

The disciples asked Jesus about the "end times", or the "sign of His coming", and " the end of the world", some versions read, "the end of the age".

The following is from Matthew 24 (All scriptures will be from the King James 1611 version):

Matthew 24:1- 3
"And Jesus went out, and departed from the temple: and his disciples
came to *him* for to shew him the buildings of the temple.
And Jesus said unto them, See ye not all these things? Verily I say unto you, there shall not

be left here one stone upon another, that shall not be thrown down. And as He sat upon the mount of Olives, the disciples came unto Him privately, saying, "Tell us, when shall these things be, and what *shall be* the sign of thy coming, and of the end of the world?"

"And as He went out of the temple, one of His disciples saith unto Him, "Master, see what manner of stones and what buildings *are here*!" And Jesus answering said unto them, "Sees thou these great buildings? There shall not be left one stone upon another, that shall not be thrown down." Mark 13: 1,2

There are many historical accounts on this matter, starting around 70 AD (Anno Domini), some call it 70 CE (Common Era), when this prophecy was fulfilled.

There are at least 100 Biblical prophecies that Jesus Christ fulfilled, I will mention a couple here: Genesis 3: 15, "And I will put enmity between thee and the woman, and between thy seed and her seed;..." This is the first mention of His virgin birth. Women do not have "seeds", we have eggs. This is what many believe to be the first mention of the virgin birth, and I happen to agree with them. The verse goes on to say, "...it shall bruise thy head, and thou shalt bruise his heal." God was speaking to the serpent in the Garden of Eden after the fall of Adam and Eve. This prophecy was about the crucifixion, where Jesus suffered a death blow from the enemy, the devil, but Jesus did not stay dead, and in turn it was actually a death blow to the devil because now the sin debt was paid in full and mankind did not have to live as slaves to sin anymore. To kill a snake, you need to "crush his head" and Jesus did that at the "place of the skull" (Matt. 27:33, Mk.15:22; John 19:17). Also, Isaiah 7:13, 14 plainly tells of Jesus' virgin birth. The scriptures that confirm His virgin birth many years later, are these: Matthew 11:18-23 and Luke 1:26-35.

Jesus would be born in the lineage of King David: 2 Samuel 7:12,13; Isaiah 9:7; this was fulfilled in: Matthew 1:1; Luke 1:32; and confirmed again in Acts 13:22,23.

And one more prophecy: Psalm 22:16; Zechariah 12:10, tell of His hands and feet being pierced, and in Matthew 27:35; John 20:25-29, this was confirmed.

This is just the beginning!

For more information on fulfilled Bible Prophecies, you can go online to the site: http://bibleprobe. com/365messianicprophecies.htm .

There are about 300 or more prophecies that Jesus Christ fulfilled with His birth to His ascension, and if He fulfilled all of those with no mistakes, I am sure that all of the "End Time" prophecies will also be fulfilled with no mistakes. The only question is, will we be ready, or will we miss out, just like the religious sects in Jesus' day? They should have known and been ready for His arrival. He is coming back just like He said, make no mistake about it. He also said to watch and pray.

How many Bible prophecies in the Old Testament are you aware of that have been fulfilled?

_____

_____

"These things I have spoken unto you, that in me ye might have peace. In the world ye shall have **tribulation**: but be of good cheer; I have overcome the world." ~ John 16:33

What does "tribulation" mean? I am so glad you asked. Here is the definition according to *Strong's:

tribulation (G 2347); θλῖψις **thlîpsis,** thlip'-sis; from G2346; pressure (literally or figuratively):—afflicted(-tion), anguish, burdened, persecution, tribulation, trouble.

> 1.a pressing, pressing together, pressure
> 2. metaph. oppression, affliction, tribulation, distress, straits

G 2346: θλίβω **thlíbō,** thlee'-bo; akin to the base of G5147; to crowd (literally or figuratively):—afflict, narrow, throng, suffer tribulation, trouble.

The first time the word ""tribulation" is mentioned is found in Deuteronomy 4:30

> "When thou art in **tribulation**, and all these things are come upon thee, *even* in the **latter days**, if thou turn to the LORD thy God, and shalt be obedient unto his voice;"

In the Hebrew it means: (H 6862);öÇø **tsar,** tsar; or öÈø tsâr; from H6887; narrow; (as a noun) a tight place (usually figuratively, i.e. trouble); also a pebble (as in H6864); (transitive) an opponent (as crowding):—adversary, afflicted(-tion), anguish, close, distress, enemy, flint, foe, narrow, small, sorrow, strait, tribulation, trouble.

The first time it is mentioned in the New Testament, is found in Matthew 13:21, which reads as the following:

> "Yet hath he not root in himself, but dureth for a while: for when **tribulation** or persecution ariseth because of the word, by and by He is offended."

In this verse it means the following:

(G 2347); θλῖψις **thlîpsis,** thlip'-sis; from G2346; pressure (literally or figuratively):—afflicted(-tion), anguish, burdened, persecution, tribulation, trouble.

Persecution is part of the definition. We will see persecution and tribulations, and it will become more intense before the LORD comes back. Here are some more verses on this subject:

John 16:33
"These things I have spoken unto you, that in me ye might have peace. In the world ye shall have **tribulation**: but be of good cheer; I have overcome the world."

Acts 14:22
"Confirming the souls of the disciples, *and* exhorting them to continue in the faith, and that we must through much **tribulation** enter into the kingdom of God."

Romans 5:3
"And not only *so*, but we glory in tribulations also: knowing that **tribulation** worketh patience;"

Romans 8:35
"Who shall separate us from the love of Christ? *shall* **tribulation**, or distress,
or persecution, or famine, or nakedness, or peril, or sword?"

Romans 12: 12
"Rejoicing in hope; patient in **tribulation**; continuing instant in prayer;"

2 Corinthians 1:4
"Who comforteth us in all our **tribulation**, that we may be able to comfort them which
are in any trouble, by the comfort wherewith we ourselves are comforted of God."

2 Corinthians 7:4
"Great *is* my boldness of speech toward you, great *is* my glorying of you: I am
filled with comfort, I am exceeding joyful in all our **tribulation**."

1 Thessalonians 3:4
"For verily, when we were with you, we told you before that we should
suffer **tribulation**; even as it came to pass, and ye know."

2 Thessalonians 1:6
"Seeing *it is* a righteous thing with God to recompense **tribulation** to them that trouble you;"

Of course, there are many more scriptures than these; but, did you notice something they all have in common?

Not one of them say we will not suffer tribulation. I know some say, "But there is a difference between tribulation and GREAT tribulation.

Let's look at how many times the word **"great tribulation"** is used:

Matthew 24:21 "For then shall be **great tribulation**, such as was not since the beginning of the world to this time, no, nor ever shall be."

Revelation 2:22 "Behold, I will cast her into a bed, and them that commit adultery with her into **great tribulation,** except they repent of their deeds."

Revelation 7:14 "And I said unto him, Sir, thou knowest. And he said to me, These are they which came out of **great tribulation**, and have washed their robes, and made them white in the blood of the Lamb."

In these verses, the words "great" and "tribulation" are defined seperately, so let's take a look at these words:

great : (G 3173); μέγας **mégas,** meg'-as; (including the prolonged forms, feminine μεγάλη megálē, plural μεγάλοι megáloi, etc.; compare also G3176, G3187); big (literally or figuratively, in a very wide application):—(+

fear) exceedingly, great(-est), high, large, loud, mighty, + (be) sore (afraid), strong, × to years.

tribulation: (G 2347); θλῖψις **thlîpsis,** thlip'-sis; from G2346; pressure (literally or figuratively):—afflicted(-tion), anguish, burdened, persecution, tribulation, trouble.

There is another "end time" word used in the Holy Bible, and it is the word, "wrath". Let's see how it is used in the Holy scriptures, and how it compares to "tribulation" or even "great tribulation".

There are many scriptures concerning the word "wrath"; but I will choose a few to share and if you want, you can do a word search on this word and see how it is applied; but for now, here are a few:

"Let no man deceive you with vain words: for because of these things cometh the **wrath** of God upon the children of disobedience." Ephesians 5:6

"For which things' sake the **wrath** of God cometh on the children of disobedience:" Colossians 3:6

"And to wait for his Son from heaven, whom he raised from the dead, *even* Jesus, which delivered us from the **wrath** to come." 1 Thessalonians 1:10

"For God hath not appointed us to **wrath**, but to obtain salvation by our Lord Jesus Christ," 1 Thessalonians 5:9

"And said to the mountains and rocks, Fall on us, and hide us from the face of him that sitteth on the throne, and from the **wrath** of the Lamb: For the great day of his wrath is come; and who shall be able to stand?" Revelation 6:16,17

"And I saw another sign in heaven, great and marvelous, seven angels having the seven last plagues; for in them is filled up the **wrath** of God." Revelation 15:1 And here it what this word means in the *Strong's:

Wrath: (G 3709); ὀργή **orgḗ,** or-gay'; from G3713; properly, desire (as a reaching forth or excitement of the mind), i.e. (by analogy), violent passion (ire, or (justifiable) abhorrence); by implication punishment:—anger, indignation, vengeance, wrath.

G 3713: ὀρέγομαι **orégomai,** or-eg'-om-ahee; middle voice of apparently a prolonged form of an obsolete primary (compare G3735); to stretch oneself, i.e. reach out after (long for):—covet after, desire.

From reading this definition, I tend to think that even in God's wrath, it's a form of love reaching out to set His creation straight and draw them unto Himself. God is good and He starts out being so kind and He is always generous, but when people begin to take His kindness for granted and begin to misplace their thankfulness and worship, He corrects them gently with words of correction, and if they refuse, then He uses more severe measures. Eventually, some will repent. Unfortunately, there are many who are hard headed and hard heart-ed. Why would we want to break God's heart and grieve Him? It is because of sin, that we live in such a fallen world with so many problems, but it is our choice. We ultimately decide where our eternal soul goes. For the record, not everyone will make it to Heaven. If you are reading this right now, and you are not 100% sure where you will spend eternity, talk to God and ask Him to forgive your sins and make Him the LORD of your life. We are not guaranteed our next breath so, **now** is the time to make the best decision you will ever make, by making Him the LORD of your life.

Before going any further, let's have a quick review:

In case you are new to the Bible, the Old Testament was written in Hebrew, and the New Testament was written in Greek; this is why the definitions are defined in Hebrew for the Old Testament and in Greek for the NewTestament.

(* Strong's is short for Strong's Exhuastive Concordance; and I will be using bold print for emphasis.)

REVIEW

1. In the Strong's Hebrew (H 2856) definition of the word "sealed": what is something this word means:

_____

2. In the Strong's Greek (G 2347) definition, the word "tribulation" means:

_____

_____

3. Will God's children/ people, go through any kind of tribulation? _____

4. Will God's children be under God's wrath? _____

5. Is there a difference between "tribulation" and "great tribulation"? _____

6. Is there a difference between "great tribulation" and the "wrath of God"? _____

_____

7. What is the difference between "great tribulation" and the "wrath of God"?
if you see a difference:

_____

_____

8. Is God harsh by pouring out His wrath or is He just and merciful?

_____

_____

_____

9. According to Colossians 3:6 and Eph. 5:6, who does God's wrath come upon?

_____

10. According to 1 Thessalonians 1:10, who delivered us from the wrath to come?

_____

CHAPTER 2

In this section of the Bible study, I want us to look at a few more definitions and then dive deeper into the Holy Word of God, but first, let's open this study with prayer.

Dear Heavenly Father,
we thank You, for Your awesome gift of salvation through Your Son, Jesus Christ.
We thank You for loving us and adopting us as Your dear children. Jesus, thank You for calling us friends and revealing to us, by Your Spirit, what we need to know in these times, in which we are living. Thank You, Holy Spirit, for leading us into all Truth.
You have good plans for us and we desire to fulfill Your destiny that You have for us.
May we walk in Your Truth and be obedient to Your Word.
In Jesus name, we humbly pray and give You thanks. Amen.

"And Jesus answered and said unto them, Take heed that no man deceive you."
Matthew 24:4

Jesus Christ does not want us to be deceived. He is the Truth (John 14:6). For the record, not everyone is a child of God. In John 8:44, Jesus is talking to some of the religious people in His day, and He said: "Ye are of *your* father the devil, and the lusts of your father ye will do. He was a murderer from the beginning, and abode not in the truth, because there is no truth in him. When he speaketh a lie, he speaketh of his own: for he is a liar, and the father of it."

Jesus also said that He knows His own, implying that not everyone is His. Even though Jesus was speaking to the Jews during His day, the Jews did not kill Jesus Christ. You can't kill the very essence of Life. Jesus said that no man can take His life from Him. Look at John 10:17, 18 :

"Therefore doth my Father love me, because I lay down my life, that I might take it again.
No man taketh it from me, but I lay it down of myself. I have power to lay it down,
and I have power to take it again. This commandment have I received of my Father."

On the pages13,14 I would like to present to you the scriptures that run parallel to each other describing what can be expected in the end times. We will look an examine these scriptures more closely.

Matthew	Mark
Matthew "For many shall come in my name, saying, I am Christ; and shall deceive many." Matthew 24:5	Mark "For many shall come in my name, saying, I am Christ; and shall deceive many." Mark 13:6
"And ye shall hear of wars and rumors of wars: see that ye be not troubled: for all these things must come to pass, but the end is not yet." Matthew 24:6	"And when ye shall hear of wars and rumours of wars, be ye not troubled: for such things must needs be; but the end shall not be yet." Mark 13:7
"For nation shall rise against nation, and kingdom against kingdom: and there shall be famines, and pestilences, and earthquakes, in divers places. All these are the beginning of sorrows." Matthew 24:7,8	"For nation shall rise against nation, and kingdom against kingdom: and there shall be earthquakes in divers places, and there shall be famines and troubles: these are the beginnings of sorrows." Mark 13:8
"Then shall they deliver you up to be afflicted, and shall kill you: and ye shall be hated of all nations for my name's sake. And then shall many be offended, and shall betray one another, and shall hate one another. And many false prophets shall rise, and shall deceive many. And because iniquity shall abound, the love of many shall wax cold. But he that shall endure unto the end, the same shall be saved. And this gospel of the kingdom shall be preached in all the world for a witness unto all nations; and then shall the end come." Matthew 24:9-14	"But take heed to yourselves: for they shall deliver you up to councils; and in the synagogues ye shall be beaten: and ye shall be brought before rulers and kings for my sake, for a testimony against them. And the gospel must first be published among all nations. But when they shall lead you, and deliver you up, take no thought beforehand what ye shall speak, neither do ye premeditate: but whatsoever shall be given you in that hour, that speak ye: for it is not ye that speak, but the Holy Ghost. Now the brother shall betray the brother to death, and the father the son; and children shall rise up against their parents, and shall cause them to be put to death. And ye shall be hated of all men for my name's sake: but he that shall endure unto the end, the same shall be saved." Mark 13:9-13
"Immediately after the tribulation of those days shall the sun be darkened, and the moon shall not give her light, and the stars shall fall from heaven, and the powers of the heavens shall be shaken: And then shall appear the sign of the Son of man in heaven: and then shall all the tribes of the earth mourn, and they shall see the Son of man coming in the clouds of heaven with power and great glory. And he shall send his angels with a great sound of a trumpet, and they shall gather together his elect from the four winds, from one end of heaven to the other. Now learn a parable of the fig tree; When his branch is yet tender, and putteth forth leaves, ye know that summer is nigh: So likewise ye, when ye shall see all these things, know that it is near, even at the doors." Matthew 24:29-33	"But in those days, after that tribulation, the sun shall be darkened, and the moon shall not give her light, And the stars of heaven shall fall, and the powers that are in heaven shall be shaken. And then shall they see the Son of man coming in the clouds with great power and glory. And then shall he send his angels, and shall gather together his elect from the four winds, from the uttermost part of the earth to the uttermost part of heaven. Now learn a parable of the fig tree; When her branch is yet tender, and putteth forth leaves, ye know that summer is near: So ye in like manner, when ye shall see these things come to pass, know that it is nigh, even at the doors." Mark 13:24-29

Luke	Revelation
"And he said, Take heed that ye be not deceived: for many shall come in my name, saying, I am Christ; and the time draweth near: go ye not therefore after them." Luke 21:8	"And I saw, and behold a white horse: and he that sat on him had a bow; and a crown was given unto him: and he went forth conquering, and to conquer." Revelation 6:2
"But when ye shall hear of wars and commotions, be not terrified: for these things must first come to pass; but the end is not by and by." Luke 21:9	"And there went out another horse that was red: and power was given to him that sat thereon to take peace from the earth, and that they should kill one another: and there was given unto him a great sword." Revelation 6:4
"Then said he unto them, Nation shall rise against nation, and kingdom against kingdom: And great earthquakes shall be in divers places, and famines, and pestilences; and fearful sights and great signs shall there be from heaven." Luke 21:10,11	"And I heard a voice in the midst of the four beasts say, A measure of wheat for a penny, and three measures of barley for a penny; and see thou hurt not the oil and the wine. And I looked, and behold a pale horse: and his name that sat on him was Death, and Hell followed with him. And power was given unto them over the fourth part of the earth, to kill with sword, and with hunger, and with death, and with the beasts of the earth." Revelation 6:6,8
"But before all these, they shall lay their hands on you, and persecute you, delivering you up to the synagogues, and into prisons, being brought before kings and rulers for my name's sake. And it shall turn to you for a testimony. Settle it therefore in your hearts, not to meditate before what ye shall answer: For I will give you a mouth and wisdom, which all your adversaries shall not be able to gainsay nor resist. And ye shall be betrayed both by parents, and brethren, and kinsfolks, and friends; and some of you shall they cause to be put to death. And ye shall be hated of all men for my name's sake. But there shall not an hair of your head perish. In your patience possess ye your souls." Luke 21:12-19	"And when he had opened the fifth seal, I saw under the altar the souls of them that were slain for the word of God, and for the testimony which they held: And they cried with a loud voice, saying, How long, O Lord, holy and true, dost thou not judge and avenge our blood on them that dwell on the earth? And white robes were given unto every one of them; and it was said unto them, that they should rest yet for a little season, until their fellow servants also and their brethren, that should be killed as they were, should be fulfilled." Revelation 6:9-11
"And there shall be signs in the sun, and in the moon, and in the stars; and upon the earth distress of nations, with perplexity; the sea and the waves roaring; Men's hearts failing them for fear, and for looking after those things which are coming on the earth: for the powers of heaven shall be shaken. And then shall they see the Son of man coming in a cloud with power and great glory. And when these things begin to come to pass, then look up, and lift up your heads; for your redemption draweth nigh. And he spake to them a parable; Behold the fig tree, and all the trees; When they now shoot forth, ye see and know of your own selves that summer is now nigh at hand. So likewise ye, when ye see these things come to pass, know ye that the kingdom of God is nigh at hand. Verily I say unto you, this generation shall not pass away, till all be fulfilled." Luke 21:25-32	"And I beheld when he had opened the sixth seal, and, lo, there was a great earthquake; and the sun became black as sackcloth of hair, and the moon became as blood; And the stars of heaven fell unto the earth, even as a fig tree casteth her untimely figs, when she is shaken of a mighty wind. And the heaven departed as a scroll when it is rolled together; and every mountain and island were moved out of their places. And the kings of the earth, and the great men, and the rich men, and the chief captains, and the mighty men, and every bondman, and every free man, hid themselves in the dens and in the rocks of the mountains; And said to the mountains and rocks, Fall on us, and hide us from the face of him that sitteth on the throne, and from the wrath of the Lamb: For the great day of his wrath is come; and who shall be able to stand?" Revelation 6:12-17

In the previous pages, I showed a comparison of scriptures and how they seem to parallel with each other. I left a few verses out on purpose, and I do plan on coming back to them, later on in this study. I did the comparisons to show you the harmony of these scriptures and how they are referring to the same things. If you read them, you can see the similarities. With that being said, the "beginning of sorrows", as mentioned in Matthew 24:8 and Mark 13:8, have the same components as found in Revelation 6:1-8.

Matthew 24:9,10, is clearly still in alignment with Revelation 6:9-11. I really am convinced that Matthew 24 just gives details that Mark 13, Luke 21, and Revelation 6 do not give, but at the same time, these other books reveal a few things that Matthew 24 didn't cover.

In the Gospel of John, we do not read any of these end time events, but when we come to the book of Revelation we read more than we could have ever have imagined. Just as all four Gospels give an account of the life of Christ, His death, and His resurrection, they all give an account of what will happen in the last days, before His return, or before He calls us Home. I would not be surprised if Matthew 24:11 is speaking of the "fake news" we keep hearing about, and many are listening to, in our day.

In the next verse, verse 12, it says that :

"And because iniquity shall abound, the love of many shall wax cold."

The word "iniquity" is another word for "lawlessness". Look at the uprising of lawlessness, de-funding the police, and such evil atrocities today! I would dare say 20-30 years ago, you would not have seen these things. 40-50 years ago, the police force and the law were respected. Have there been evil acts committed by some in the law enforcement agencies? Yes, and when they were caught they were punished, as they should be, but rioting, looting, and committing more crimes, like today, does not fix or solve anything. Instead, it makes things worse.

Lawlessness, is clearly an act of the devil. That old serpent is out to kill, steal, and destroy (John 10:10). The Lord said we would know people by their fruit (Luke 6:43-45). We are living in very dangerous times. That's why we must look to the LORD, now more than ever. His perfect love can cast out fear, and He is able to keep us until He calls us Home.

I am persuaded that Revelation 6:14 is of the same time frame that Matthew 24:30,31; Mark 13:26,27, and when Luke 21:27,28 happens. I believe it's a clue to what we will see before we are out of here.

The Lord doesn't want us to be deceived, He states this many times throughout scripture. Now, let's look at some more verses in Matthew chapter 24, starting with verse 4 and discover some more words and their meanings, to get a better understanding of what our LORD was saying:

In Matthew 24:4, Jesus said, "...Take heed that no man deceive you." Let's look at the words, "heed" and "deceive":

Heed: (G 991); βλέπω **blépō**, blep'-o; a primary verb; to look at (literally or figuratively):—behold, beware, lie, look (on, to), perceive, regard, see, sight, take heed.

Deceive : (G 4105); πλανάω **planáō,** plan-ah'-o; from G4106; to (properly, cause to) roam (from safety, truth, or virtue):—go astray, deceive, err, seduce, wander, be out of the way. G 4106: πλάνη **plánē,** plan'-ay; feminine of G4108 (as abstractly); objectively, fraudulence; subjectively, a straying from orthodoxy or piety:—deceit, to deceive, delusion, error.

It's so easy to read scripture and think we know and understand it, until we see what some of what the words actually mean. That's why I have so many definitions in this book.

Let's look at some more words and their meanings found in Matthew 24:6:

> "And ye shall hear of wars and rumors of wars: see that ye be not troubled:
> for all *these things* must come to pass, but the end is not yet."

wars: (G 4171); πόλεμος **pólemos,** pol'-em-os; from πέλομαι pélomai (to bustle); warfare (literally or figuratively; a single encounter or a series):—battle, fight, war.

rumours : (G 189); ἀκοή **akoế,** ak-o-ay'; from G191; hearing (the act, the sense or the thing heard):—audience, ear, fame, which ye heard, hearing, preached, report, rumor. G 191; ἀκούω **akoúō,** ak-oo'-o; a primary verb; to hear (in various senses):—give (in the) audience (of), come (to the ears), (shall) hear(-er, -ken), be noised, be reported, understand.

troubled: (G 2360); θροέω **throeó,** thro-eh'-o; from θρέομαι thréomai to wail; to clamor, i.e. (by implication) to frighten:—trouble.

> Verse 7: "For nation shall rise against nation, and kingdom against kingdom: and
> there shall be famines, and pestilences, and earthquakes, in divers places."

nation: (G 1484); ἔθνος **éthnos,** eth'-nos; probably from G1486; a race (as of the same habit), i.e. a tribe; specially, a foreign (non-Jewish) one (usually, by implication, pagan):—Gentile, heathen, nation, people.

kingdom: (G 932); βασιλεία **basileía,** bas-il-i'-ah; from G935; properly, royalty, i.e. (abstractly) rule, or (concretely) a realm (literally or figuratively):—kingdom, + reign

1. royal power, kingship, dominion, rule
    1. not to be confused with an actual kingdom but rather the right or authority to rule over a kingdom
    2. of the royal power of Jesus as the triumphant Messiah
    3. of the royal power and dignity conferred on Christians in the Messiah's kingdom
4. a kingdom, the territory subject to the rule of a king
5. used in the N.T. to refer to the reign of the Messiah

famines: (G 3042); λιμός **limós,** lee-mos'; probably from G3007 (through the idea of destitution); a scarcity of food:—dearth, famine, hunger. G 3007; λείπω **leípō,** li'-po; a primary verb; to leave, i.e. (intransitively or passively) to fail or be absent:—be destitute (wanting), lack.

pestilences: (G 3061); λοιμός **loimós,** loy'-mos; of uncertain affinity; a plague (literally, the disease, or figuratively, a pest):—
pestilence(-t).

I read in Wikipedia, where a "pest" is described as "any animal or plant detrimental to humans or human concerns". The term is particularly used for creatures that damage crops, livestock and forestry, or cause a nuisance to people, especially in their homes. Right now, as I am writing this, there is a big deal on the Corona Virus going on, and I found this more interesting on what Wikipedia had under the section titled, "Concept":

A pest is any living thing, whether animal, plant or fungus, which humans consider troublesome to themselves, their possessions or the environment.[1] It is a loose concept, as an organism can be a pest in one setting but beneficial, domesticated or acceptable in another. Microorganisms, whether bacteria, microscopic fungi, protists, or viruses that cause trouble, on the other hand, are generally thought of as causes of disease (pathogens) rather than as pests.[2] An older usage of the word "pest" is of a deadly epidemic disease, specifically plague. In its broadest sense, a pest is a competitor to humanity.[3]

Reference # 1."What is a pest?". Commonwealth of Australia: Department of Health. 1 November 2010. Retrieved 13 May 2020.
Reference # 2. "Pests and pathogens". Julius Kühn-Institut: Federal Research Centre for Cultivated Plants. Retrieved 13 May 2020.
Reference # 3. Merriam-Webster dictionary, accessed 22 August 2012.

With that in mind, I do believe we are seeing these things going on in our world today. As I am writing this, there is some strange weather that has hit California. They are having Firenadoes! These are said to be: "among the rarest weather phenomena on Earth"! (https://www.breakingisraelnews.com/156811/ freak-summer-fire-ice-hail-storm-hits-california-just-like-in-exodus/?fbclid=IwAR1Lf92E8dRzfHV_ 3k8CB8v4ozvlNauJDFhrXRdLuRCnFk7DdiPDedxjA34)

Are you still not convinced that we are living in the "Last Days"?

Then there are the "earthquakes":

Earthquakes: (G 4578); σεισμός **seismós,** sice-mos'; from G4579; a commotion, i.e. (of the air) a gale, (of the ground) an earthquake:—earthquake, tempest. G 4579; σείω **seíō,** si'-o; apparently a primary verb; to rock (vibrate, properly, sideways or to and fro), i.e. (generally) to agitate (in any direction; cause to tremble); figuratively, to throw into a tremor (of fear or concern):—move, quake, shake.

"All these *are* the beginning of sorrows."
Matthew 24:8

sorrows: (G 5604); ὠδίν **ōdín,** o-deen'; akin to G3601; a pang or throe, especially of childbirth:—pain, sorrow, travail.

G 3601; ὀδύνη **odýnē,** od-oo'-nay; from G1416; grief (as dejecting):—sorrow.

"Then shall they deliver you up to be afflicted, and shall kill you: and
ye shall be hated of all nations for my name's sake."
Matthew 24:9

afflicted: (G 2347); θλῖψις **thlîpsis,** thlip'-sis; from G2346; pressure (literally or figuratively):—afflicted(-tion), anguish, burdened, persecution, tribulation, trouble. G 2346; θλίβω **thlíbō,** hlee'-bo; akin to the base of G5147; to crowd (literally or figuratively):—afflict, narrow, throng, suffer tribulation, trouble.

shall kill: (G 615); ἀποκτείνω **apokteínō,** ap-ok-ti'-no; from G575 and κτείνω kteínō (to slay); to kill outright; figuratively, to destroy:—put to death, kill, slay.

hated: (G 3404); μισέω **miséō,** mis-eh'-o; from a primary μῖσος mîsos (hatred); to detest (especially to persecute); by extension, to love less:—hate(-ful).

name's sake: (G 3686); ὄνομα **ónoma,** on'-om-ah; from a presumed derivative of the base of G1097 (compare G3685); a "name" (literally or figuratively) (authority, character):—called, (+ sur-)name(-d).

In the outline of this word "name's sake", beside II, it says this: the name is used for everything which the name covers, everything the thought or feeling of which is aroused in the mind by mentioning, hearing, remembering, the name, i.e. for one's rank, authority, interests, pleasure, command, excellences, deeds etc.

I found that to be interesting. Continuing on:

iniquity: (G 458);ἀνομία **anomía,** an-om-ee'-ah; from G459; illegality, i.e. violation of law or (genitive case) wickedness:—iniquity, × transgress(-ion of) the law, unrighteousness. G 459; ἄνομος **ánomos,** an'-om-os; from G1 (as a negative particle) and G3551; lawless, i.e. (negatively) not subject to (the Jewish) law; (by implication, a Gentile), or (positively) wicked:—without law, lawless, transgressor, unlawful, wicked.

I am giving you these definitions, so you can see for yourselves, what they mean. We need to study for ourselves, so we will not be deceived.

shall wax cold (G 5594); ψύχω **psýchō,** psoo'-kho; a primary verb; to breathe (voluntarily but gently, thus differing on the one hand from G4154, which denotes properly a forcible respiration; and on the other from the base of G109, which refers properly to an inanimate breeze), i.e. (by implication, of reduction of temperature by evaporation) to chill (figuratively):—wax cold.

"But he that shall endure unto the end, the same shall be saved."
Matthew 24:13

he that shall **endure :** (G 5278); ὑπομένω**hypoménō,** hoop-om-en'-o; from G5259 and G3306; to stay under (behind), i.e. remain; figuratively, to undergo, i.e. bear (trials), have fortitude, persevere:—abide, endure, (take) patient(-ly), suffer, tarry behind.

the end: (G 5056); τέλος **télos,** tel'-os; from a primary τέλλω téllō (to set out for a definite point or goal); properly, the point aimed at as a limit, i.e. (by implication) the conclusion of an act or state (termination (literally, figuratively or indefinitely), result (immediate, ultimate or prophetic), purpose); specially, an impost or levy (as paid):—+ continual, custom, end(-ing), finally, uttermost.

shall be saved: (G 4982); σώζω **sṓzō,** sode'-zo; from a primary σῶς sōs (contraction for obsolete σάος sáos, "safe"); to save, i.e. deliver or protect (literally or figuratively):—heal, preserve, save (self), do well, be (make) whole.

Many have different thoughts on what "the end" is, some think that we have to endure to the end of the world. I guess that could be true, but when a person dies, isn't that "the end of the world" for them? Feel free to discuss this with your group. By the time this gets published, you may have to discuss it by video.

One day it seems like we are able to have a small group, and another day we are not. Some states are allowed to have group gatherings, and other states are not, because of the Covid -19 virus.

I guess it depends on where you are located. In any case, I hope you will be able to discuss this and pray about it.

FEEDBACK

I know I have given a LOT of definitions, but, I am hoping that it will help clear up some questions about what was being said here. On page 17, can you see the difference between nation and kingdom?

"Nation" seems to be referring to the countries of the world. Kingdom seems to imply that "Christians" will be fighting with one another. I believe we have been seeing this, and it looks like it may become worse as time goes on.

Do you think that we have seen an increase in famines in the last 15-20 years?

Have we witnessed anything that would be considered a "pestilence" in the last 10 years?

What do you think would be considered a "pestilence"?

2 Peter 3:10 says:

"But the day of the Lord will come as a thief in the night; in the which the heavens
shall pass away with a great noise, and the elements shall melt with fervent heat,
the earth also and the works that are therein shall be burned up."

fervent heat: (G 2741); καυσόω **kausóō,** kow-so'-o; from G2740; to set on fire:—fervent heat.
G 2740; καῦσις **kaûsis,** kow'-sis; from G2545; burning (the act):—be burned.
G 2545; καίω **kaíō,** kah'-yo; apparently a primary verb; to set on fire, i.e. kindle or (by implication) consume:—burn, light.

So, it sounds like everything is going to get burned up one day, how's that for global warming?

Here, in 2 Peter, it also states that the LORD will come as a thief in the night, but it says the heavens will pass away with a **great noise**. Aren't thieves quiet? Does this sound contradictory? Think of it this way, thieves come when no one is looking for them. It does not mean they do not make any noise. Have you ever seen a house or a car that thieves broke into? What a mess! I am sure that when my car was broken into, a number of years ago, it wasn't quiet. Breaking glass is a little on the loud side.

That doesn't seem very quiet to me. What do you suppose it means by the "elements" in 2 Peter 3:10?
the elements: (G 4747); στοιχεῖον **stoicheîon,** stoy-khi'-on; neuter of a presumed derivative of the base of G4748; something orderly in arrangement, i.e. (by implication) a serial (basal, fundamental, initial) constituent (literally), proposition (figuratively):—element, principle, rudiment.

I. any first thing, from which the others belonging to some series or composite whole take their rise, an element, first principal

A. the letters of the alphabet as the elements of speech, not however the written characters, but the spoken sounds

B. the elements from which all things have come, the material causes of the universe

C. the heavenly bodies, either as parts of the heavens or (as others think) because in them the elements of man, life and destiny were supposed to reside

D. the elements, rudiments, primary and fundamental principles of any art, science, or discipline

1.i.e. of mathematics, Euclid's geometry

1 Thessalonians 4:16 :
"For the Lord himself shall descend from heaven with a shout, with the voice of the archangel, and with the trumpet of God: and the dead in Christ shall rise first:"

Shouting and a trumpet doesn't sound very quiet to me. Let's take a look at the meaning of the words, "shout" and "trumpet" and see what these mean in the Greek:

shout: (G 2752);κέλευμα **kéleuma,** kel'-yoo-mah; from G2753; a cry of incitement:—shout.

In the outline of Biblical usage, found in the Blue Letter Bible, it is stated:
an order, command, spec. a stimulating cry, either that by which animals are roused and urged on by man, as horses by charioteers, hounds by hunters, etc., or that by which a signal is given to men, e.g. to rowers by the master of a ship, to soldiers by a commander (with a loud summons, a trumpet call).

trump: (G 4536); σάλπιγξ **sálpinx,** sal'-pinx; perhaps from G4535 (through the idea of quavering or reverberation); a trumpet:—trump(-et).

REVIEW

1. What is it that Jesus said to take heed or beware of in Matthew 24:4?

_____

2. Jesus said that, though we may hear of wars and rumours or wars, what was not yet to be?
3. What is one definition of famine?
4. What is one definition of pestilence ? _____

_____

5. According to the Greek word of "sorrows" (G 5604); what kind of pain/ sorrow is this?

_____

6. According to the word "afflicted": (G 2347), name 3 words used to describe this:

_____   _____   _____

7. In the word "hated" (G 3404), what was the definition under number one? _____

8. Under the second definition of iniquity (G 3551), what was the first word used to describe this?

_____

9. According to the definition of enduring to the end, what does that mean?

_____

10. According to 2 Peter 3:10, what will one day happen to this Earth, that we are currently living on?

_____

_____

11. In 1 Thessalonians 4: 16, what two sounds are made at the LORD's return?

_____   _____

12. Who is going to rise first in the "rapture"; or, when the LORD meets us in the air?

_____

_____

CHAPTER 3

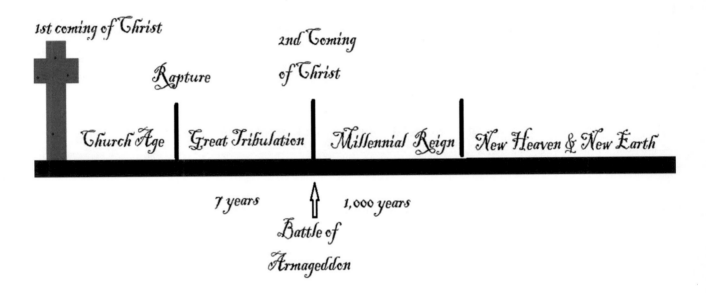

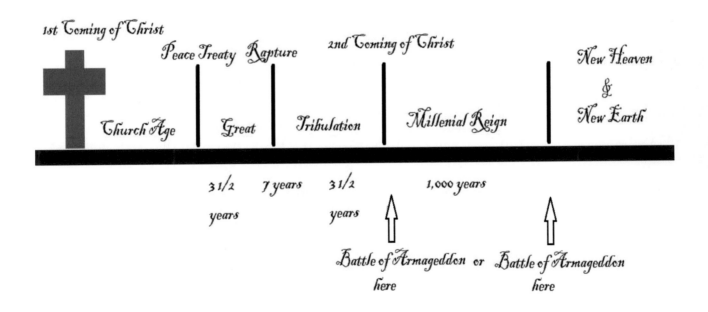

The first chart, is the most popular one concerning a "Pre-Tribulation Rapture" of the Church. The second time line, or chart, is the one concerning a "Mid-Tribulation Rapture" of the Church. The next one. I am about to present to you is a mix of "Mid-Tribulation Rapture" and a "Post Tribulation Rapture", of the Church, it is a "Post Tribulation/ Pre-Wrath Tribulation" of the Church. The funny thing is, everyone has scriptures for their ideas/ beliefs, yet they do not all agree. I would like to point out that this is not God's fault. God is not the author of confusion. It is God's Holy Word that becomes watered down through man's religion and filtered through fallen human mindsets. That is why it is always good to ask God what His Word says and not just accept whatever someone else says. I have heard a lot of good teaching on the "End Times", but what got me interested in the subject matter was what happened to me, way back in my early childhood days. God spoke to me about this time frame and revealed stuff to me, that I kept in my heart and pondered them internally...until now.

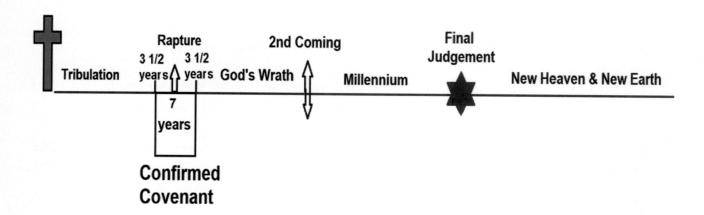

If you are doing this Bible study and are unfamiliar with the definitions of "Pre -Trib" or "Pre-Tribulation", "Mid-Trib" (aka: Mid-Tribulation), or Post Tribulation (aka: Post Trib), let me take some time now to explain these definitions briefly for you. Many believe that there will be a time frame of 7 years for a "Tribulation" spoken of in the Bible. Some call it the "7 Year Great Tribulation". Truth is, the Bible never says that there will be a 7 year tribulation or 7 years of great tribulation. The people speaking of this get the idea from a passage in Daniel 9:27, which says this:

"And he shall confirm the covenant with many for one week:
and in the midst of the week he shall cause the sacrifice and the oblation to cease,
and for the overspreading of abominations he shall make *it* desolate,
even until the consummation, and that determined shall be poured upon the desolate."

If you read this, you will see the very first line where " shall confirm the covenant with many for one week". You may ask, "How do they get years out of a week?" I am glad you asked.
Scripture can interpret scripture, if we look back and read Daniel 9:2, we will find our first clue:

"In the first year of his reign I, Daniel understood by books the number of
the years, whereof the word of the LORD came to Jeremiah the prophet, that
he would accomplish seventy years in the desolation of Jerusalem."

This is referring to Jeremiah 25:11,12, and Jeremiah 29:10. Then in Daniel 9:24, which says:

"Seventy weeks are determined upon thy people and upon thy holy city, to finish the transgression,
and to make an end of sins, and to make reconciliation for iniquity, and to bring in everlasting
righteousness, and to seal up the vision and prophecy, and to anoint the most Holy."

The word "weeks" in this verse is this:

H 77620;ùŃÈáåÌòÇ **shâbûwa'**, shaw-boo'-ah; or ùŃÈáËòÇ shâbua'; also (feminine) ùŃÀáËòÈä shebu'âh;
properly, passive participle of H7650 as a denomative of H7651; literally, sevened, i.e. a week (specifically,
of years):—seven, week.

The word "Rapture" is not in the Bible. We get this word from 1 Thessalonians 4:17,

"Then we which are alive *and* remain shall be caught up together with them in the
clouds, to meet the Lord in the air: and so shall we ever be with the Lord."

The phrase "caught up", is in Latin "rapio" according to Thayer's Greek Lexicon, also found at: https://
www.blueletterbible.org/lang/lexicon/lexicon.cfm?Strongs=G726&t=KJV

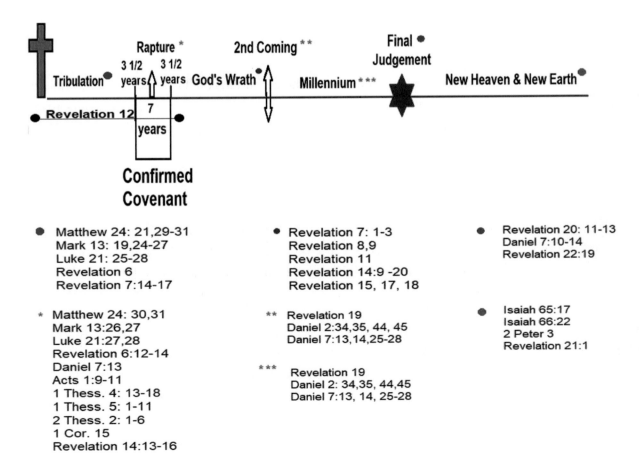

Matthew 24: 21,29-31
Mark 13: 19,24-27
Luke 21: 25-28
Revelation 6
Revelation 7:14-17

* Matthew 24: 30,31
Mark 13:26,27
Luke 21:27,28
Revelation 6:12-14
Daniel 7:13
Acts 1:9-11
1 Thess. 4: 13-18
1 Thess. 5: 1-11
2 Thess. 2: 1-6
1 Cor. 15
Revelation 14:13-16

Revelation 7: 1-3
Revelation 8,9
Revelation 11
Revelation 14:9 -20
Revelation 15, 17, 18

** Revelation 19
Daniel 2:34,35, 44, 45
Daniel 7:13,14,25-28

*** Revelation 19
Daniel 2: 34,35, 44,45
Daniel 7:13, 14, 25-28

Revelation 20: 11-13
Daniel 7:10-14
Revelation 22:19

Isaiah 65:17
Isaiah 66:22
2 Peter 3
Revelation 21:1

Also, the breaking of the covenant, "in the midst of the week", mentioned in Daniel 9:27 coincides with Revelation 11:2,6,14; and Revelation 13:5.

For the most part when people speak of the "Great Tribulation" or the "7 years of Great Tribulation", it is so spooky and scary. That's because they mix it with the "Wrath of God".

God's obedient children are not under God's wrath (John 3:36; Romans 1:18; Romans 2:1-10; Colossians 3:6; 1 Thessalonians 1:10; and 1 Thessalonians 5:9). Some say that, if you are not saved you will spend eternity in Hell, this is not true. You will spend eternity in the Lake of Fire (Revelation 20:14,15). Heaven and the New Jerusalem are also getting mixed up by many (Revelation 3: 12: Revelation 21:2). They are actually, two different places. The same thing has happened with the "Great Tribulation" and the "Wrath of God".

For the record, there is no place in the Holy Bible that says that there will be 7 years of Great Tribulation. The seven years is about a confirmed covenant, but it gets broken mid-way through. Seeing what we learned about persecution and tribulation, is there any place in the Bible, that excludes us from these?

As you can see, that God's wrath is something we do not want, and if we remain faithful to Him, I believe we will most certainly escape that, according to the scriptures. Praise the LORD!

Time is short and we need to make sure we are ready for His soon return, it is closer now than it ever has been!

1 John 2:18
"Little children, it is the last time: and as ye have heard that antichrist shall come,
even now are there many antichrists; whereby we know that it is the last time."

1 Thessalonians 3:4
"For verily, when we were with you, we told you before that we should
suffer tribulation; even as it came to pass, and ye know."

Let's look at the word "antichrists" / "antichrist", in 1 John 2: 18:
antichrist : (G 500); ἀντίχριστος **antíchristos,** an-tee'-khris-tos; from G473 and G5547; an opponent of the Messiah:—antichrist

As you may have noticed, I added Revelation 12 to my [4th] timeline. Revelation chapter 12 is very interesting. God is not the author of confusion, He is a God of order. Everything in Revelation is in order. Let me give you a few examples of what I mean:

"I, John, who also am your brother, and companion in tribulation,
and in the kingdom and patience of Jesus Christ, was in the isle that is called Patmos,
for the word of God, and for the testimony of Jesus Christ.
I was in the Spirit on the Lord's day, and heard behind me a great voice, as of a trumpet,
Saying, I am Alpha and Omega, the first and the last: and,
What thou seest, write in a book, and send *it* unto the seven churches which are in Asia;
unto Ephesus, and unto Smyrna, and unto Pergamos, and unto Thyatira,

and unto Sardis, and unto Philadelphia, and unto Laodicea."
Revelation 1:9-11

"Unto the angel of the church of Ephesus write; These things saith he that holdeth
the seven stars in his right hand, who walketh in the midst of
the seven golden candlesticks;"
Revelation 2:1

"And unto the angel of the church in Smyrna write;
These things saith the first and the last,
which was dead, and is alive;"
Revelation 2:8

"And to the angel of the church in Pergamos write;
These things saith he which hath the sharp sword with two edges;"
Revelation 2:12

"And unto the angel of the church in Thyatira write; These things saith the Son of God,
who hath his eyes like unto a flame of fire, and his feet *are* like fine brass;"
Revelation 2:18

"And unto the angel of the church in Sardis write;
These things saith he that hath the seven Spirits of God, and the seven stars;
I know thy works, that thou hast a name that thou livest, and art dead."
Revelation 3:1

"And to the angel of the church in Philadelphia write; These things saith he that is holy,
he that is true, he that hath the key of David, he that openeth,
and no man shutteth; and shutteth, and no man openeth;"
Revelation 3:7

"And unto the angel of the church of the Laodiceans write;
These things saith the Amen, the faithful and true witness,
the beginning of the creation of God;"
Revelation 3:14

If God started the book of Revelation in order, why would He mix it up later in the book? All these churches were in the order as He mentioned them in Revelation 1:11. He began everything in proper order at the time of creation as well. God began His work in darkness, but in order for it's manifestation, it needed light. So, He first spoke forth light into being. He separated the two, further creating order. Plants need water and soil, God had the water there to start His creation then He called for dry land, this He did before creating plant life. Animals need water and plants, this is why they were created soil and water, before the plants, and the plants, before the animals, etc. God knows what He is doing and He does everything in order. I want this point to be understood because, so many times people seem to understand that God is the God of order, **_until_**...the book of Revelation. If you have read His Holy Word, you may recall that He is the God Who changes not.

"For I *am* the LORD, I change not"
Malachi 3:6

"Jesus Christ the same yesterday, and to day, and for ever."
Hebrews 13:8

Prior to Revelation 12, we have the obvious Revelation chapters 1-11, but there are some interesting things going on in chapters 1-11 that seem to flow together until we get to chapter 12. Here is an outline to explain what I mean:(Rev. 1) Introduction

> 1. Revealing of Jesus Christ
>   B. the author
>   C. to whom this was written to
> 2. (Rev. 2,3) Letters to the 7 churches
> 3. (Rev. 4) John in the Spirit before the throne
> 4. (Rev. 5) The Book with 7 seals
> 5. (Rev.6) The Lamb opens the 1ˢᵗ six Seals
> 6. (Rev.7) Two groups of people
>   A. On Earth (Rev. 7:1-8)
>   B. In Heaven (Rev. 7:9-17)
> 7. (Rev. 8) 7ᵗʰ Seal opened and 7 Trumpets begin
> 8. (Rev. 9) 5ᵗʰ Angel with trumpet and 3 woes begin
> 9. (Rev. 10) John eats the book
> 10. (Rev. 11) 2ⁿᵈ woe and 7ᵗʰ angel begins to blow

And this brings us to Revelation chapter 12. Revelation 12, almost seems out of place.

Jesus spoke to John in Revelation 1:19 and said,

"Write the things which thou hast seen, and the things which are,
and the things which shall be hereafter;"

Revelation 12 is all of these in one. This chapter shows the birth, death, and resurrection of Jesus Christ. John witnessed most of that, and he spent time with Mary (John 19:27), so, this would follow under the things he had seen. The things which are, of course, Jesus "being caught up to His throne" (Rev. 12:5). The rest is yet to come. I will explain this debatable theory:

There is a short time frame given to the woman who "fled into the wilderness" (Rev. 12:6; 3 ½ years). Right now, the devil is the Prince of the power of the air (Eph.2:2). If you are not sure about that, check out the news, T.V. programs, movies, music...etc. You see there are 3 Heavens: Highest Heaven or third Heaven where God dwells; 2ⁿᵈ Heaven – outer space, and 1ˢᵗ Heaven, the sky, where the birds fly (2 Cor. 12:2; Genesis 1:14-18,20).

Right now, the devil walks about as a roaring lion seeking whom he may devour (1 Peter 5:8). He walks to and fro throughout the Earth (Job 1:6; 2:1); but, he will be cast down to the Earth. This is when he decides to take over with the 7 year confirmed covenant and breaks it (Daniel 9:27; Revelation 11:2; Revelation 12:6, and Revelation 13:5). The devil comes down full of wrath, the King James puts it this way, "...Woe to the inhabitors of the earth and of the sea! For the devil is come down unto you, having great wrath, because he knoweth that he hath but a short time."

If the devil had been cast down thousands of years ago, it wouldn't have been "a short time", especially, since the time frame is given in verse 6 and again in verse 14. The same expression is used in Daniel 12:7, as in Revelation 12:14.

There is a woman in Revelation 12 that many are divided on who she is, some say the woman is the Church, some say she is Israel, and I have heard someone say they think she is Mary. Let's look at some thought provoking questions and see what the possibilities are. Be warned, thought provoking questions can cause people to get offended rather than consider different possibilities.

Revelation 12:
1. The woman is clothed with the sun, and the moon was under her feet, and upon her head were twelve stars. This woman is in outer space, according to this and giving birth to a male child.
she is not birthing many children at this time... this is important. Later on, in verse 17 the devil makes war with the "remnant of her seed".
Verse 17 states that they are those: "...which keep the commandments of God, **and** have the testimony of Jesus Christ." This is clearly the "Saved", "Redeemed", Jews and Gentiles alike (Ephesians 2:8-22).
I am about to submit to you another possibility. Just pray about all these things and consider one more possibility, we will pick this up in the next chapter.

REVIEW

True or False

1. All Christian Millennial teachings are the same. _____

2. The scriptures clearly state that there will be a 7 year tribulation or Great Tribulation time frame.

   _____

3. The 7 year time frame comes from Daniel 9:27, and it's a "confirmed covenant".

4. The covenant gets broken in the middle of 7 years. _____

5. Daniel is the only place mentioning 42 months or 3 ½ years. _____

6. Antichrist, means: an opponent of the Messiah. _____

7. There's no difference between "tribulation" and "wrath". _____

8. God is not the author of confusion. _____

9. God is the God of order. _____

10. Revelation 12 seems different than chapters 1-11. _____

11. What are 3 ideas of who the woman in Revelation 12 are:

   _____   _____   _____

12. What three items did the woman have, that made her appear to be in space?

   _____   _____   _____

13. Who was the baby that the woman gave birth to in Revelation 12?

   _____

14. Did the woman have any other children? _____

15. Who was waiting to devour the Woman's seed? _____

CHAPTER 4

"And she brought forth a man child, who was to rule all nations with a rod of iron:
and her child was caught up unto God, and to his throne." Revelation 12:5

In this verse, we see the woman gives birth to Jesus Christ. The "Church" did not "birth Christ"; however, Christ, did start the Church. (Psalm 2:9; Matthew 16:18)

In Revelation 12:17, "And the dragon was wroth with the woman,
and went to make war with the remnant of her seed,
which keep the commandments of God, and have the testimony of Jesus Christ."

This verse could mean Israel; but, all of Israel are not believers. The "Woman" would be Israel, if not for all of her children/ seed are believers? It did say the "remnant". So, it could be Israel. The way it is worded, sounds like this could be Jew and Gentile believers. That's why some think this is the "Church", but the "Church" did not give birth to Christ, Christ "birthed the Church", or created/established the church. I would like to offer another option, not popular, but a possibility. Let's now look at a verse that I left out. It has to do with the time frame:

"And the woman fled into the wilderness, where she hath a place prepared of God,
that they should feed her there a thousand two hundred and threescore days."
Revelation 12:6

If you divide 1,260 days by 365 (days in a year), it comes to:3.4520...; rounded to 3.5 years. Is Israel only a nation for 3 ½ years?

Here are some more definitions that may shed some light on the subject:
woman: (G 1135);γυνή **gynē,** goo-nay'; probably from the base of G1096; a woman; specially, a wife:— wife, woman.

Let's go to Genesis to look further into this word and see if there are any clues in the beginning of the Bible. (For the record, according to scripture, Mary did not stay a virgin: Mat. 13:56; Mk. 6:3. She also needed a Savior:Luke 1:46-48).

"In the beginning, God created the heaven and the earth.
And the earth was without form, and void; and darkness was upon the face of the deep.
And the Spirit of God moved upon the face of the waters." Genesis 1:1,2

God: (H 430); àÁìÉäÄéí **'ĕlôhîym,** el-o-heem'; plural of H433; gods in the ordinary sense; but specifically used (in the plural thus, especially with the article) of the supreme God; occasionally applied by way of deference to magistrates; and sometimes as a superlative:—angels, × exceeding, God (gods) (-dess, -ly), × (very) great, judges, × mighty.

Spirit: (H 7307); øåÌçÇ **rûwach,** roo'-akh; from H7306; wind; by resemblance breath, i.e. a sensible (or even violent) exhalation; figuratively, life, anger, unsubstantiality; by extension, a region of the sky; by resemblance spirit, but only of a rational being (including its expression and functions):—air, anger, blast, breath, × cool, courage, mind, × quarter, × side, spirit(-ual), tempest, × vain, (whirl-) wind(-y).

In the Blue Letter Bible, they often give an outline with these definitions, and under roman numeral one, by the letter G, is this definition: "Spirit of God, the third person of the triune God, the Holy Spirit, co-equal, co-eternal with the Father and the Son", just wanted to make note of this because I want to make sure that we are on the "same page" and know Who we are talking about.

Moved: (H 7363); øÈçÇó **râchaph,** raw-khaf'; a primitive root; to brood; by implication, to be relaxed:—flutter, move, shake.
In the outline on this one, it states: I. (Qal) to grow soft, relax ; and, II. (Piel) to hover

In the Blue Letter Bible, it also has a Gesenius' Hebrew-Chaldee Lexicon, which gives the comparison of a mother hen or eagle, or a bird, that broods over her eggs. It even stated it is "...to soothe a child (as a mother)."
Are you seeing this? Are you getting this?

When the Bible goes through a geneology, it uses a term, in the King James, "begat" and here is what that words means:

begat: (H 3205); éÈìÇä **yâlad,** yaw-lad'; a primitive root; to bear young; causatively, to beget; medically, to act as midwife; specifically, to show lineage:—bear, beget, birth(-day), born, (make to) bring forth (children, young), bring up, calve, child, come, be delivered (of a child), time of delivery, gender, hatch, labour, (do the office of a) midwife, declare pedigrees, be the son of, (woman in, woman that) travail(-eth, -ing woman).

With that definition in mind, let's look at the birth of Jesus Christ.

"Now the birth of Jesus Christ was on this wise: When as his mother Mary was espoused to Joseph, before they came together, she was found with child of the Holy Ghost."
Matthew 1:18

"And the angel answered and said unto her, The Holy Ghost shall come upon thee, and the power of the Highest shall overshadow thee: therefore also that holy thing which shall be born of thee shall be called the Son of God."
Luke 1:35

As we know another word for the Holy Ghost/ Holy Spirit, is Comforter.

"But the Comforter, *which is* the Holy Ghost, whom the Father will send in my name,
He shall teach you all things, and bring all things to your remembrance,
whatsoever I have said unto you."
John 14:26

Let's break down John 14:26 and examine it :

Comforter: (G 3875); παράκλητος **paráklētos,** par-ak'-lay-tos; an intercessor, consoler:—advocate, comforter.

Holy: (G 40); ἅγιος**hágios,** hag'-ee-os; from ἄγος hágos (an awful thing) (compare G53, G2282); sacred (physically, pure, morally blameless or religious, ceremonially, consecrated):—(most) holy (one, thing), saint.

Ghost: (G 4151);πνεῦμα **pneûma,** pnyoo'-mah; from G4154; a current of air, i.e. breath (blast) or a breeze; by analogy or figuratively, a spirit, i.e. (human) the rational soul, (by implication) vital principle, mental disposition, etc., or (superhuman) an angel, demon, or (divine) God, Christ's spirit, the Holy Spirit:—ghost, life, spirit(-ual, -ually), mind.

The Father: (G 3962); πατήρ **patēr,** pat-ayr'; apparently a primary word; a "father" (literally or figuratively, near or more remote):—father, parent.

He: (G 1565); ἐκεῖνος **ekeînos,** ek-i'-nos; fromG1563; that one (or (neuter) thing); often intensified by the article prefixed:—he, it, the other (same), selfsame, that (same, very), × heir, × them, they, this, those. See also G3778.

G 3778; οὗτος **hoûtos,** hoo'-tos; from the article G3588 and G846; the **he (she or it),** i.e. this or that (often with article repeated):—he (it was that), hereof, it, she, such as, the same, these, they, this (man, same, woman), which, who.

There are a lot of scriptures speaking of the Holy Ghost/Holy Spirit and use the term "He"; here is another example of this found in John 16:13:

"Howbeit when He, the Spirit of truth, is come, He will guide you into all truth:
for He shall not speak of himself; but whatsoever He shall hear,
that shall He speak: and He will shew you things to come."

More definitions:

He: (G 1565); ἐκεῖνος **ekeînos,** ek-i'-nos; from G1563; that one (or (neuter) thing); often intensified by the article prefixed:—he, it, the other (same), **selfsame,** that (same, very), × their, × them, they, this, those. See also G3778.

G 3778; οὗτος **hoûtos,** hoo'-tos; from the article G3588 and G846; the **he (she or it),** i.e. this or that (often with article repeated):—he (it was that), hereof, it, she, such as, the same, these, they, **this (man, same, woman),** which, who.

Spirit: (G 4151); πνεῦμα **pneûma,** pnyoo'-mah; from G4154; a current of air, i.e. breath (blast) or a breeze; by analogy or figuratively, a spirit, i.e. (human) the rational soul, (by implication) vital principle, mental disposition, etc., or (superhuman) an angel, demon, or (divine) God, Christ's spirit, the Holy Spirit:—ghost, life, spirit(-ual, -ually), mind. Compare G5590.

He will guide: (G 3594); ὁδηγέω **hodēgéō,** hod-ayg-eh'-o; from G3595; to show the way (literally or figuratively (teach)):—guide, lead.

*He shall: (G 2980); λαλέω **laléō,** lal-eh'-o; a prolonged form of an otherwise obsolete verb; to talk, i.e. utter words:—preach, say, speak (after), talk, tell, utter.

(*"He shall" is part of the whole phrase: "He shall not speak")

Himself: (G 1438); ἑαυτοῦ **heautoû,** heh-ow-too'; from a reflexive pronoun otherwise obsolete and the genitive case (dative case or accusative case) of G846; **him- (her-, it-, them-,** also (in conjunction with the personal pronoun of the other persons) my-, thy-, our-, your-) self (selves), etc.:—alone, **her (own, -self), (he) himself,** his (own), itself, one (to) another, our (thine) own(-selves), + that she had, their (own, own selves), (of) them(-selves), they, thyself, you, your (own, own conceits, own selves, -selves).

> I. himself, herself, itself, themselves

> "For God so loved the world, that He gave His only begotten Son,
> that whosoever believeth in Him should not perish, but have everlasting life."
> John 3:16

only begotten: (G 3439); μονογενής **monogenḗs,** mon-og-en-ace'; from G3441 and G1096; only-born, i.e. sole:—only (begotten, child).

> "Wherefore I desire that ye faint not at my tribulations for you, which is your glory.
> For this cause I bow my knees unto the Father of our Lord Jesus Christ,
> Of whom the whole family in heaven and earth is named,
> That he would grant you, according to the riches of his glory,
> to be strengthened with might by his Spirit in the inner man;"
> Ephesians 3:13-16

> "But he, being full of the Holy Ghost, looked up steadfastly into heaven,
> and saw the glory of God, and Jesus standing on the right hand of God,"
> Acts 7:55

> "And the Holy Ghost descended in a bodily shape like a dove upon Him,
> and a voice came from heaven, which said, Thou art my beloved Son;
> in Thee I am well pleased." Luke 3:22

> "And the LORD God said, *It is* not good that the man should be alone;
> I will make him an help meet for him...
> And the rib, which the LORD God had taken from man,

made he a woman, and brought her unto the man. And Adam said,
This *is* now bone of my bones, and flesh of my flesh:
she shall be called Woman, because she was taken out of Man.
Therefore shall a man leave his father and his mother,
and shall cleave unto his wife: and they shall be one flesh."
Genesis 2:18-24

"And he answered and said unto them, Have ye not read, that he which made them
at the beginning made them male and female, And said,
For this cause shall a man leave father and mother, and shall cleave to his wife:
and they twain shall be one flesh? Wherefore they are no more twain, but one flesh.
What therefore God hath joined together, let not man put asunder."
Matthew 19 :4-6

"For this cause shall a man leave his father and mother,
and shall be joined unto his wife, and they two shall be oneflesh."
Ephesians 5:31

"Know ye not that your bodies are the members of Christ?
shall I then take the members of Christ, and make *them* the members of an harlot?
God forbid.
What? know ye not that he which is joined to an harlot is one body?
for two, saith He, shall be one flesh."
1 Corinthians 6:15,16

"For there are three that bear record in heaven,
the Father, the Word, and the Holy Ghost:
and these three are one."
1 John 5:7

So, with all that said, here is one more possibility. The Holy Spirit/Holy Ghost is like the Mother, and of course we have Father God, and God the Son, which is the **only begotten** Son of God. We can become sons and daughters of God; but we are adopted...Jesus is the ONLY begotten Son, we have to be born again, we are adopted and then we become joint-heirs with Christ Jesus. It is a spiritual birth for us, but Jesus Christ is God. He is Spirit and He is fully human.

"And will be a Father unto you, and ye shall be my sons and daughters, saith the Lord Almighty."
2 Corinthians 6:18

"But as many as received Him, to them gave He power
to become the sons of God, *even* to them that believe on His name:"
John 1:12

"And because ye are sons, God hath sent forth the Spirit of His

Son into your hearts, crying, Abba, Father."
Galatians 4:6

"For as many as are led by the Spirit of God, they are the sons of God.
For ye have not received the spirit of bondage again to fear;
but ye have received the Spirit of adoption, whereby we cry, Abba, Father.
The Spirit itself beareth witness with our spirit, that we are the children of God:
And if children, then heirs; heirs of God, and joint-heirs with Christ;
if so be that we suffer with *Him*, that we may be also glorified together.
For I reckon that the sufferings of this present time
are not worthy *to be compared* with the glory which shall be revealed in us.
For the earnest expectation of the creature waiteth
for the manifestation of the sons of God."
Romans 8:14-19

I know that some will not like this; but, it is a strong possibility.

I submit to you to consider that there are three persons of the Divinity: Father God, Mother God, and their Son, Jesus Christ, the only begotten Son of God, and these three are One.

If this is the case, then the woman in Revelation 12, could very well be, the Holy Spirit of God. Holy Spirit gave birth to Jesus Christ, and we (the born-again Believers) are Her seed, the Jew first, and also the Gentiles. There is only One Way to Heaven, to the Father (John 14:6), and that is through Jesus Christ and through His perfect blood sacrifice.
There is only one door to enter into Heaven (John 10:7-9). There is no other way, there is no other name given (Acts 4:12).

"For as in Adam all die, even so in Christ shall all be made alive."
1 Corinthians 15:22

"And so it is written, The first man Adam was made a living soul;
the last Adam *was made* a quickening spirit."
1 Corinthians 15:45

"Wherefore I desire that ye faint not at my tribulations for you, which is your glory.
For this cause I bow my knees unto the Father of our Lord Jesus Christ,
Of whom the whole family in heaven and earth is named,
That He would grant you, according to the riches of his glory,
to be strengthened with might by His Spirit in the inner man;"
Ephesians 3:13-16

Please know this, that the plan of salvation is through Jesus Christ and His perfect sacrifice. This pleased the Father. It also pleases the Father when we accept His free gift. It cost Christ everything to bring us salvation. Are you a part of the family of God? You can be, by accepting His gift, His blood sacrifice for your sins. Please don't wait any longer.

REVIEW

1. The woman in Revelation 12 gave birth to _____

2. According to Strong's what is the definition of the word "woman"?

_____

3. In Genesis 1;1,2, the name for God in the Hebrew "àÁìÉäÄéí'elohiym" is it in the singular or plural when used here? _____

4. Give one definition of the word "Spirit" as found in Strong's (H 7307), on page 33:

_____

5. Give a definition on the word "moved" according to Strong's (H 7363):

_____

6. In the **Gesenius' Hebrew-Chaldee Lexicon,** what two animals are mentioned as brooding over their young or over their eggs?

_____

7. On pages 33 and 35, is there a difference between the word "spirit" and ghost"?

8. Also, on page 35, under "Comforter", what does the Comforter do?

_____

9. In the Greek, when the word "he" is used; does it always mean a male, or could it be a "she"?

_____

_____

10. What does "only begotten" mean (page 37)? _____

_____

CHAPTER 5

"And there appeared another wonder in heaven; and behold a great red dragon,
having seven heads and ten horns, and seven crowns upon his heads."
Revelation 12:3

"And I will put enmity between thee and the woman, and between thy seed
and her seed; it shall bruise thy head, and thou shalt bruise his heel."
Genesis 3:15

"And there appeared a great wonder in heaven; a woman clothed with the sun,
and the moon under her feet, and upon her head a crown of twelve stars:
And she being with child cried, travailing in birth, and pained to be delivered.
And there appeared another wonder in heaven; and behold a great red dragon,
having seven heads and ten horns, and seven crowns upon his heads. And his tail drew the
third part of the stars of heaven, and did cast them to the earth: and the dragon stood before
the woman which was ready to be delivered, for to devour her child as soon as it was born."
Revelation 12:1-3

"And the great dragon was cast out, that old serpent, called the Devil, and Satan,
which deceiveth the whole world: he was cast out into the earth,
and his angels were cast out with him."
Revelation 12:9

Scripture always confirms scripture. If you have a Bible that is contradictory, please get another Bible. There
are no contradictions in God's Holy Word. For the record, some have misunderstood His Word and thought
there were contradictions. Seek God, His Holy Spirit will lead you into all Truth.

(*The dragon/ the devil, is always after our "seed" or, if you will, our children.)

"And there appeared another wonder in heaven; and behold a great red dragon,
having seven heads and ten horns,
and seven crowns upon his heads." Revelation 12:3

I would like to call this the, "Fall of the Dragon".

Beloved, we have been through a lot of test & trials.
We have many battle scars to show our encounters with the enemy. A lot of our loved ones have suffered
great ordeals because of the onslaught of the enemy.

Today, we see so much violence, so much hatred, and I dare say, it will only get worse as time goes on.

Our enemy is not flesh and blood...our enemy is this dragon, who tempts us and accuses us on a regular basis.

Although, we can be our worse enemy at times, the real culprit behind the scene is the low down snake, hiding undercover, and making forbidden fruit as beautiful as ever.

I don't dare give him too much credit, but I don't want to make light of him either.
This enemy is dangerous. Although, he is not a lion, he goes about as one, seeking whom he may devour.
Lies and deception are his main weapons.
We have to beware of his schemes, but we can't do that if we don't know them.
All Believers need to ask God for discernment. This enemy is all about dividing and conquering.
The truth about a deceiver is that he will play both sides of the field.

Try to get someone into unity with a multitude, like at the tower of Babel, or just simply agree with anyone that doesn't agree with God. That's why it is very important to have a relationship with God, have Christ in our hearts, His Spirit leading us and guiding us. If we are not led by the Holy Spirit, then it is the wrong spirit that we're agreeing with. For the record, God never goes against His Holy Word.

One day, our adversary will be put in his place, but so will all those who have followed him, instead of Christ.

I for one, prefer to be on the side of Christ and not the Dragon.

This second wonder that appears in the heavens, is a great red dragon. He wanted to devour the "seed" of the woman. Let's take a closer look at some more words:

devour: (G2719);κατεσθίω **katesthíō**, kat-es-thee'-o; from G2596 and G2068 (including its alternate); to eat down, i.e. devour (literally or figuratively):—devour.
https://www.blueletterbible.org/lang/lexicon/lexicon.cfm?Strongs=G2719&t=KJV the following is from the out line under :

II. Metaph.
A. to devour i.e. squander, waste: substance
B. to devour i.e. forcibly appropriate: widows' property
C. to strip one of his goods
   1. to ruin (by the infliction of injuries)
D. by fire, to devour i.e. to utterly consume, destroy
E. of the consumption of the strength of body and mind by strong emotions

Great: (G 3173);μέγας **mégas,**meg'-as; (including the prolonged forms, feminine μεγάλη megálē, plural μεγάλοι megáloi, etc.; compare also G3176, G3187); big (literally or figuratively, in a very wide application):— (+ fear) exceedingly, great(-est), high, large, loud, mighty, + (be) sore (afraid), strong, × to years.

Wonder: (G 4592); σημεῖον **sēmeîon**, say-mi'-on; neuter of a presumed derivative of the base of G4591; an indication, especially ceremonially or supernaturally:—miracle, sign, token, wonder.

G 4591; σημαίνω **sēmaínō**, say-mah'-ee-no; from σῆμα sēma (a mark; of uncertain derivation); to indicate:—signify.

Heaven: (G 3772); οὐρανός **ouranós**, oo-ran-os'; perhaps from the same as G3735 (through the idea of elevation); the sky; by extension, heaven (as the abode of God); by implication, happiness, power, eternity; specially, the Gospel (Christianity):—air, heaven(-ly), sky.

So, in heaven/space, we have a sign or wonder; of a woman that gives birth to a male child and a dragon that is big, possibly loud, mighty, strong, and afraid. I think he is afraid of the woman's seed and that's why he wants to "devour" her seed. I do not want to give too many opinions in this study, but maybe this would be a good point to stop, pray about it, and or discuss it. What do you think?

Now, back to this crazy looking dragon. The Bible says he has 7 heads and 10 horns, and it says that the dragon was "red". So, that raises a lot of questions, like: Why is the dragon red? Why does it have 10 horns; but, only 7 heads? In verse 9 of Revelation 12, it tells us *who* this dragon is.

Now to go into why "red" and all these heads and horns. Numbers, colors, symbols, they all represent something, kind of like the American flag. We're going to look into all the symbolism later on in this chapter. But first, there's something very familiar about this "dragon". The first thing we notice is that this "dragon" was the same "serpent" that was in the Garden of Eden:

"And the great dragon was cast out, that old serpent, called the Devil, and Satan, which deceiveth
the whole world: he was cast out into the earth, and his angels were cast out with him."
Revelation 12:9

"Thou hast been in Eden the garden of God; every precious stone was thy covering,
the sardius, topaz, and the diamond, the beryl, the onyx, and the jasper,
the sapphire, the emerald, and the carbuncle, and gold:
the workmanship of thy tabrets and of thy pipes was prepared in thee
in the day that thou wast created."
Ezekiel 28:13

"Now the serpent was more subtle than any beast of the field which the LORD God had made.
And he said unto the woman, Yea, hath God said,
Ye shall not eat of every tree of the garden?"
Genesis 3:1

"And the LORD God said unto the serpent, Because thou hast done this,
thou art cursed above all cattle, and above every beast of the field;
upon thy belly shalt thou go, and dust shalt thou eat all the days of thy life:"
Genesis 3:14

"And I will put enmity between thee and the woman, and between thy seed
and her seed; it shall bruise thy head, and thou shalt bruise his heel."
Genesis 3:15

It is clear that this "Dragon" is the "serpent" that tricked Eve, but he looks different here in Revelation. Let's look at this Dragon:

"And there appeared another wonder in heaven; and behold a great red dragon,
having seven heads and ten horns, and seven crowns upon his heads."
Revelation 12:3

"After this I saw in the night visions, and behold a fourth beast, dreadful and terrible, and strong exceedingly; and it had great iron teeth: it devoured and brake in pieces, and stamped the residue with the feet of it: and it was diverse from all the beasts that were before it; and it had ten horns."
Daniel 7:7

Here in Daniel 7:7, we see this fourth beast had ten horns, as did the dragon in Revelation 12, but does it have seven heads? Let's back up and count the heads of this beast.

Daniel 7, let's start in verse 4, for time's sake:

"The first *was* like a lion, and had eagle's wings: I beheld till the wings thereof were plucked, and it was lifted up from the earth, and made stand upon the feet as a man, and a man's <u>heart</u> was given to it.
And behold another beast, a second, like to a bear, and it raised up itself on one side, and *it had* three ribs in the mouth of it between the teeth of it: and they said thus unto it, Arise, devour much flesh.
After this I beheld, and lo another, like a leopard, which had upon the back of it four wings of a fowl; the beast had also four heads; and dominion was given to it. After this I saw in the night visions, and behold a fourth beast..,"
Daniel 7:4-7a

This sounds a lot like Revelation 13:1,2 :

"And I stood upon the sand of the sea, and saw a beast rise up out of the sea,
having seven heads and ten horns, and upon his horns ten crowns,
and upon his heads the name of blasphemy.
And the beast which I saw was like unto a leopard, and his feet were as *the feet* of a bear,
and his mouth as the mouth of a lion: and the dragon gave him his power,
and his seat, and great authority."

I feel strongly led to take a closer look at Revelation 12:9, and see what a few of these words mean. We already know what "great" means, so I will not do it again. We need to know who our enemy really is:

Dragon: (G 1404); δράκων **drákōn,** drak'-own; probably from an alternate form of δέρκομαι dérkomai (to look); a fabulous kind of serpent (perhaps as supposed to fascinate):—dragon.

Was cast out: (G 906); βάλλω **bállō,** bal'-lo; a primary verb; to throw (in various applications, more or less violent or intense):—arise, cast (out), × dung, lay, lie, pour, put (up), send, strike, throw (down), thrust.

That old: (G 744); ἀρχαῖος **archaîos,** ar-khah'-yos; from G746; original or primeval:—(them of) old (time).
G 746; ἀρχή **archḗ,** ar-khay'; from G756; (properly abstract) a commencement, or (concretely) chief (in various applications of order, time, place, or rank):—beginning, corner, (at the, the) first (estate), magistrate, power, principality, principle, rule.
G 756; ἄρχομαι **árchomai,** ar'-khom-ahee; middle voice of G757(through the implication, of precedence); to commence (in order of time):—(rehearse from the) begin(-ning).

Serpent: (G 3789);ὄφις **óphis,** of'-is; probably from G3700 (through the idea of sharpness of vision); a snake, figuratively, (as a type of sly cunning) an artful malicious person, especially Satan:—serpent.

The Devil: (G 1228);διάβολος **diábolos,** dee-ab'-ol-os; from G1225; a traducer; specially, Satan (compare H7854):—false accuser, devil, slanderer. G 1225; διαβάλλω **diabállō,** dee-ab-al'-lo; from G1223 and G906; (figuratively) to traduce:—accuse.

Satan: (G 4567);Σατανᾶς **Satanâs,** sat-an-as'; of Chaldee origin corresponding to H4566 (with the definite affix); the accuser, i.e. the devil:—Satan.

H4566; îÇòÀáÌÈã **ma'bâd,** mah-bawd'; from H5647; an act:—work.
H 5647; òÈáÇã **'âbad,** aw-bad'; a primitive root; to work (in any sense); by implication, to serve, till, (causatively) enslave, etc.:—× be, keep in bondage, be bondmen, bond-service, compel, do, dress, ear, execute, husbandman, keep, labour(-ing man, bring to pass, (cause to, make to) serve(-ing, self), (be, become) servant(-s), do (use) service, till(-er), transgress (from margin), (set a) work, be wrought, worshipper,

> And the great dragon was cast out, that old serpent, called the Devil, and Satan,
> which deceiveth the whole world: he was cast out into the earth,
> and his angels were cast out with him."
> Revelation 12:9

deceiveth: (G 4105); πλανάω **planáō,** plan-ah'-o; from G4106; to (properly, cause to) roam (from safety, truth, or virtue):—go astray, deceive, err, seduce, wander, be out of the way.
G 4106; πλάνη **plánē,** plan'-ay; feminine of G4108 (as abstractly); objectively, fraudulence; subjectively, a straying from orthodoxy or piety:—deceit, to deceive, delusion, error.

Angels: (G 32); ἄγγελος **ággelos,** ang'-el-os; from ἀγγέλλω aggéllō (probably derived from G71; compare G34) to bring tidings; a messenger; especially an "angel"; by implication, a pastor:—angel, messenger.

Were cast out: (G 906); βάλλω **bállō,** bal'-lo; a primary verb; to throw (in various applications, more or less violent or intense):—arise, cast (out), × dung, lay, lie, pour, put (up), send, strike, throw (down), thrust. Compare G4496.

Just a note: I noticed that the words "cast out" are mentioned three times in this verse. I wonder if that's because he was cast out of the third Heaven, then the 2nd, and now is cast to the lower level, the Earth, where the first layer of Heaven is? If you would like to stop here and discuss as a group, feel free to do so. I also noticed, that the devil and Satan, in their very definition is the word, "accuser". We need to stop and let that one sink in a bit. Interestingly enough, the very next verse just comes right out and says it:

"And I heard a loud voice saying in heaven,
Now is come salvation, and strength, and the kingdom of our God, and the power of his Christ:
for the **accuser** of our brethren is cast down, which accused them before our God day and night."
Revelation 12:10

We need to remember, not to accuse our own; but instead, pray for one another. We all need prayer.

REVIEW

This is just a review over the definitions.

1. To devour, under section:II. Metaph. Section C & D, is to: _____

_____

2. Name 2 things that the word "great" can mean: _____

3. Name 2 things the word "wonder" can mean: _____

4.Name 3 places that are called "heaven":

_____   _____   _____

5. Give 3 of the defining words for "heaven":

_____   _____   _____

6. In the definition of "dragon", it said that it was a what kind of serpent? (Please circle one)

     a. ugly   b. wise   c. fabulous   d. dead

7. Give the definition of "Was cast out" according to (G 906): _____

_____

8. "That old" means the devil is too old to do anything. (True or False) _____

9. According the the Greek word entry G 3789, besides Satan, the word "serpent" can mean a malicious person. (True or False)

10. The words Satan and the Devil both are : _____

11. Not only is Satan an accuser; but, it comes from another word meaning to enslave. (True or False)

12. Please give a couple of words for deceiveth: (G 4105):

_____   _____

13. What do angels do? (It is also a part of them being a messenger):

_____

_____

CHAPTER 6

In Daniel 7, there are 4 separate beast coming out of the sea:

"And four great beasts came up from the sea, diverse one from another."
Daniel 7:3

In Revelation 13, there is one beast; but, with diverse body parts:
"And I stood upon the sand of the sea, and saw a beast rise up out of the sea,
having seven heads and ten horns, and upon his horns ten crowns,
and upon his heads the name of blasphemy. And the beast
which I saw was like unto a leopard, and his feet were as *the feet* of a bear,
and his mouth as the mouth of a lion: and the dragon gave him his power,
and his seat, and great authority."
Revelation 13:1,2
Daniel 7:4-7
"The first *was* like a **lion,** and had eagle's wings: I beheld till the wings thereof were plucked,
and it was lifted up from the earth, and made stand upon the feet as a man,
and a man's heart was given to it.
And behold another beast, a second, like to a **bear**, and it raised up itself on one side,
and *it had* three ribs in the mouth of it between the teeth of it:
and they said thus unto it, Arise, devour much flesh.
After this I beheld, and lo another, like a **leopard**,
which had upon the back of it four wings of a fowl;
the beast had also four heads; and dominion was given to it.
After this I saw in the night visions, and behold a **fourth beast**, dreadful and terrible,
and strong exceedingly; and it had great iron teeth: it devoured and brake in pieces,
and stamped the residue with the feet of it: and it *was* diverse from
all the beasts that *were* before it; and it had ten horns."
I believe we can clearly see the similarities from these verses.
Before we dive into these two passages, let's take a look at Daniel 2, the famous image:
"The king answered and said to Daniel, whose name *was* Beleshazzar,
Art thou able to make known unto me the dream which I have seen, and the interpretation thereof?
Daniel answered in the presence of the king, and said, The secret which the king hath demanded
cannot the wise *men*, the astrologers, the magicians, the soothsayers, shew unto the king; …
Thou, O king, sawest, and behold a great image. This great image, whose brightness
was excellent, stood before thee; and the form thereof *was* terrible.
This image's head *was* of fine gold, his breast and his arms of silver, his belly and his thighs of brass,

His legs of iron, his feet part of iron and part of clay.
Thou sawest till that a stone was cut out without hands, which smote the image
upon his feet *that were* of iron and clay, and brake them to pieces.
Then was the iron, the clay, the brass, the silver, and the gold, broken to pieces together, and became
like the chaff of the summer threshingfloors; and the wind carried them away, that no place was found
for them: and the stone that smote the image became a great mountain, and filled the whole earth."
Daniel 2:26,27,31-35

Interpretation:

"This *is* the dream; and we will tell the interpretation thereof before the king.
Thou, O king, *art* a king of kings: for the God of heaven hath given
thee a kingdom, power, and strength, and glory.
And wheresoever the children of men dwell, the beasts of the field and the fowls of the heaven hath
he given into thine hand, and hath made thee ruler over them all. Thou *art* this head of gold.
And after thee shall arise another kingdom inferior to thee, and another third kingdom of brass,
which shall bear rule over all the earth.
And the fourth kingdom shall be strong as iron: forasmuch as iron breaketh in pieces and
subdueth all *things*: and as iron that breaketh all these, shall it break in pieces and bruise.
And whereas thou sawest the feet and toes, part of potters' clay, and part of iron,
the kingdom shall be divided; but there shall be in it of the strength of the iron,
forasmuch as thou sawest the iron mixed with miry clay.
And *as* the toes of the feet *were* part of iron, and part of clay, *so* the
kingdom shall be partly strong, and partly broken.
And whereas thou sawest iron mixed with miry clay, they shall mingle themselves with the
seed of men: but they shall not cleave one to another, even as iron is not mixed with clay.
And in the days of these kings shall the God of heaven set up a kingdom, which shall
never be destroyed: and the kingdom shall not be left to other people, *but* it shall
break in pieces and consume all these kingdoms, and it shall stand for ever.
Forasmuch as thou sawest that the stone was cut out of the mountain without hands, and that it brake
in pieces the iron, the brass, the clay, the silver, and the gold; the great God hath made known to the
king what shall come to pass hereafter: and the dream *is* certain, and the interpretation thereof sure."
Daniel 2:36-45
I use a lot of scripture, but this is a Bible study. I do not want us
to miss any verse that will help our understanding.

As we compare Daniel 7 and Revelation 13, and now in Daniel chapter 2, we can see some similarities. Some argue that these are similar but not the same. Let's see for ourselves, the beast coming out of the sea in Daniel 7, are only 4 and they are individual beasts. In Revelation 13, these are all rolled up into one creepy looking monster.

In Daniel 2, there are 5 parts to the image that was in king Nebuchadnezzar's vision/dream. Now, comes the fun part: the image, the beast, and where are we?

So, let's start with Nebuchadnezzar's image that he saw in his dream:

Nebuchadnezzar's dream is mostly history. However, there are still the ten toes to come. We are living, right now, in the days of the feet. (Could be why life seems to stink. Just some humor.)

The head of gold was the one world under the control of Babylon (location: Iraq) and King Nebuchadnezzar was the world leader in his day.

The breast and arms were of silver, representing the one world under the control of the Medes (Media), under the leadership of Kings Darius and Ahasuerus, and under the leadership of King Cyrus of Persia (now known as Iran).

His belly and thighs were of brass; Greek Empire (location Greece), under the world leader, Alexander the Great.

Then came the Iron legs, the Roman Empire, under the leadership of the Ceasars. Rome was divided into two parts the North and the South. You can easily find this online. I have a picture for you to color on page 14.

If you remember, when Jesus walked the Earth, the Romans were the world dominating power. A lot has happened since then. There have been many wars, rumors of wars, earthquakes, and all the things Jesus said would happen in the last days, except, before He comes back again, there is the issue of the "feet and ten toes". Some say this has already happened. Jesus said that these things will happen, as in, they hadn't happened yet. Jesus was answering His disciples questions, concerning (1) When will the 2nd Temple be destroyed (the one in their day), (2) the sign of His coming, and (3) the end of the world.

The 10 toes, and the 10 horns, seem to be referring to the same time frame and the same "kings".

"And *as* the toes of the feet *were* part of iron, and part of clay,
so the kingdom shall be partly strong, and partly broken.
And whereas thou sawest iron mixed with miry clay, they shall mingle themselves with the seed of men:
but they shall not cleave one to another, even as iron is not mixed with clay.
And in the days of these kings shall the God of heaven set up a kingdom, which shall never be destroyed:
and the kingdom shall not be left to other people,
but it shall break in pieces and consume all these kingdoms, and it shall stand for ever."
Daniel 2:42-44

There is a man of God, Irvin Baxter, who pointed out that in Daniel 7:4, the beast that looked like a lion that had eagles wings, the wings were plucked off and the wings were "... made stand upon the feet as a man, and a man's heart was given to it." Irvin points out that the emblem of the United Kingdom/Great Britain, is that of a lion; America, is that of an eagle and a man (Uncle Sam); and furthermore, America left/declared her independence from Great Britain on July 4. This particular verse, just happens to be found in Daniel 7:4. I wanted to point this out because he could actually be on to something. In Revelation 13, the beast there is very similar to the beast in Daniel 7, as I had said before, but now, they are unified. For the record, there is no mention of the wings. This may be a good thing. Also, in Revelation 13, the body is of the leopard, the feet of a bear, and the mouth of the lion, as he also points out, could be referring to the main language of the day.

I looked up to see what is the most popular language in our world today, and English does appear to be one of the most dominant.

Feet would tell of the movement, in this case that of the "Bear", if it is Russia, then that would mean it is of a Communist movement. It does seem like there is a BIG push for Socialism and Communism, around the world today, including here in our wonderful USA. My prayer is we will not have to suffer through the evils of Communism in our great land.

I would like to point out that the color that best represents Communism is "red". The dragon and the beast are red in color. This also may be a clue as to where things are going.

"After this I saw in the night visions, and behold a fourth beast, dreadful and terrible, and strong exceedingly; and it had great iron teeth: it devoured and brake in pieces, and stamped the residue with the feet of it: and it *was* diverse from all the beasts that *were* before it; and it had ten horns.
I considered the horns, and, behold, there came up among them another little horn, before whom there were three of the first horns plucked up by the roots: and, behold, in this horn *were* eyes like the eyes of man, and a mouth speaking great things.
I beheld till the thrones were cast down, and the Ancient of days did sit, whose garment *was* white as snow, and the hair of his head like the pure wool: his throne *was like* the fiery flame, *and* his wheels *as* burning fire.
A fiery stream issued and came forth from before him: thousands upon thousands ministered unto him, and ten thousand times ten thousand stood before him: the judgment was set, and the books were opened."
Daniel 7:7-10

Notice the iron in the ten toes and, in this case, the iron teeth and the ten horns. Now, let's look at Revelation 12 and 13:

"And there appeared another wonder in heaven; and behold a great red dragon, having seven heads and ten horns, and seven crowns upon his heads." Revelation 12:3
"And I stood upon the sand of the sea, and saw a beast rise up out of the sea, having seven heads and ten horns, and upon his horns ten crowns, and upon his heads the name of blasphemy." Revelation 13:1

Here's the deal: I am not sure what all we will see before our LORD returns to meet us in the air, but I submit to you, that we are closer now than ever before. Even as I am writing this book, prophecies are being fulfilled, concerning the return of our Lord and Savior, Jesus Christ.

In September of 2021, the red heifer will be ready to be sacrificed. According to the scriptures, the red heifer has to be spotless, to sanctify the Temple (Numbers 19). The Sanhedrin are already making preparations for the third Temple. They have everything they need. They are training priests for their office, to do sacrifices, and all according to scripture.

You can check it out for yourself at: https://free.messianicbible.com/feature/israels-priests-prepare-third-temple/

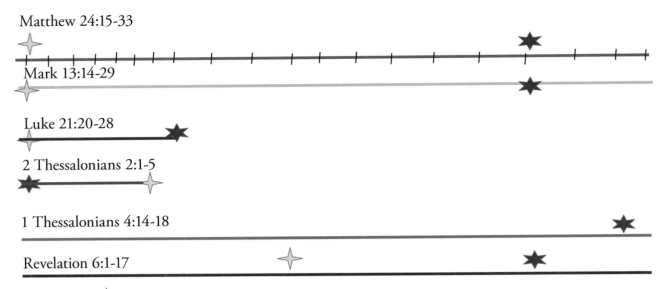

Matthew 24:15-33

Mark 13:14-29

Luke 21:20-28

2 Thessalonians 2:1-5

1 Thessalonians 4:14-18

Revelation 6:1-17

✦ -About the time the Antichrist is revealed; thus, the abomination of Desolation.
✸ -The time Jesus appears in the clouds to call us home (aka: Rapture).

Knowing that there is a difference between "Tribulation", "Great Tribulation" and time of "Wrath", wouldn't you say we are real close to our LORD coming back? Israel had to be a nation again according to prophecy, and that happened in 1948. Jerusalem is supposed to be her capital, and in 2017, this happened. The third Temple has to be rebuilt on the Temple mount in order for the Antichrist to stand in it declaring himself to be god. This is about to happen. This can be discussed further. I know it has been the debate for many years among Bible scholars. If you read the book of Revelation, you will also see that there are three different kinds of wrath:

1. The Wrath of the Lamb, 2. the wrath of the Dragon, and 3. the Wrath of God.

I cannot emphasize it enough: we need to make sure we are right with God.

He is coming back soon. The wrath of the dragon will be bad, but nothing will compare to the Lamb's wrath and/or the wrath of God.

Jesus told us in scripture to watch and pray. Beloved, we need to be doing that everyday. We are living in crazy and dangerous times, another sign of Christ's soon return. May He find us faithful and obedient to His whole Word.

God bless you all. I look forward to doing a part 2, if God tarries.

So, where are we at?

I believe we are getting real close to the trumpet sounding, and the "Rapture".

A few more things still need to happen, but we are closer now than we have ever been before.

I was having lunch with a friend of mine earlier today, and she informed me of missionaries recently discovering people on an Island that had not heard the Gospel. Now they have and are sharing

this Good News with their extended families that were on other islands.

Matthew 24:14 is being fulfilled as I am writing this:

> "And this gospel of the kingdom shall be preached in all the world
> for a witness unto all nations; and then shall the end come."

My prayer is like that found written by John, in Revelation 22:20,21:

> "He which testifieth these things saith, Surely I come quickly. Amen. Even so, come, Lord Jesus.
> The grace of our Lord Jesus Christ *be* with you all. Amen."

REVIEW

1. Are there any similarities between Daniel 2's image, Daniel 7's beast, and Revelation 13's beast? __

_____

2. What's the difference between the beast in Daniel 7 and Revelation13?

_____

_____

3. What do the 10 toes represent in the image? _____

4. Are the 10 horns in Daniel 7, the same in Revelation 13? _____

5. In the dream in Daniel 2, what 4 nations were represented?

_____   _____

_____   _____

6. Are Bible prophecies still being fulfilled today? _____

7. Is there more than one type of wrath mentioned in the Bible? _____

8. From what we have read in the Bible, are we close to the return of Christ?

_____

Are you ready for the "Rapture", to meet the LORD in the air? _____

If you answered "no" to number 9, ask God to help you get and be ready...time, one day, will run out.

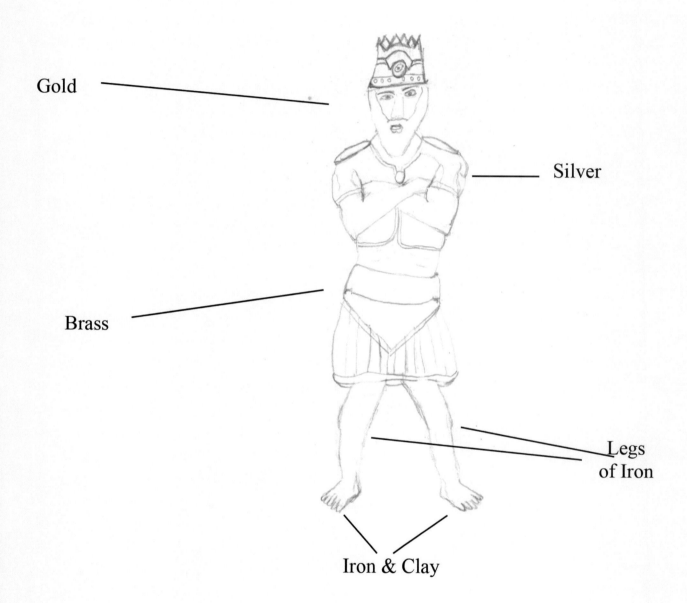

Gold

Silver

Brass

Legs
of Iron

Iron & Clay

Printed in the United States
By Bookmasters